THIS BOOK

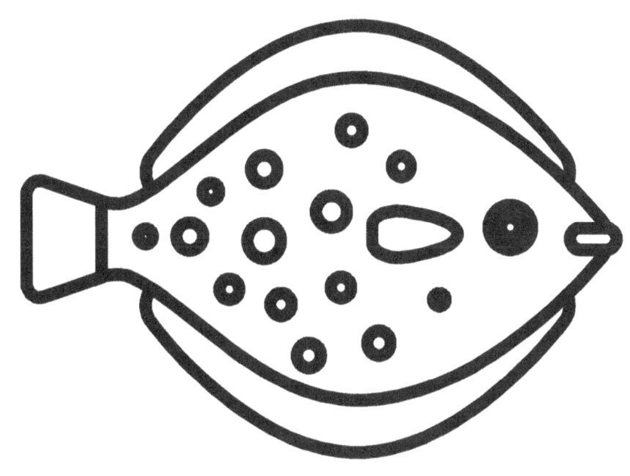

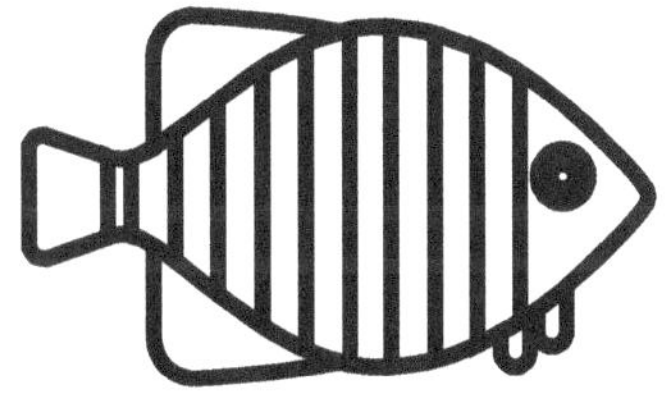

BELONGS TO

TRY TO REPEAT IT

4

5

color it

8

TRY TO REPEAT IT

FISHES

TRY TO DRAW A WHALE FROM THE PREVIOUS PAGE

PIRANHAS

12

SHARKS

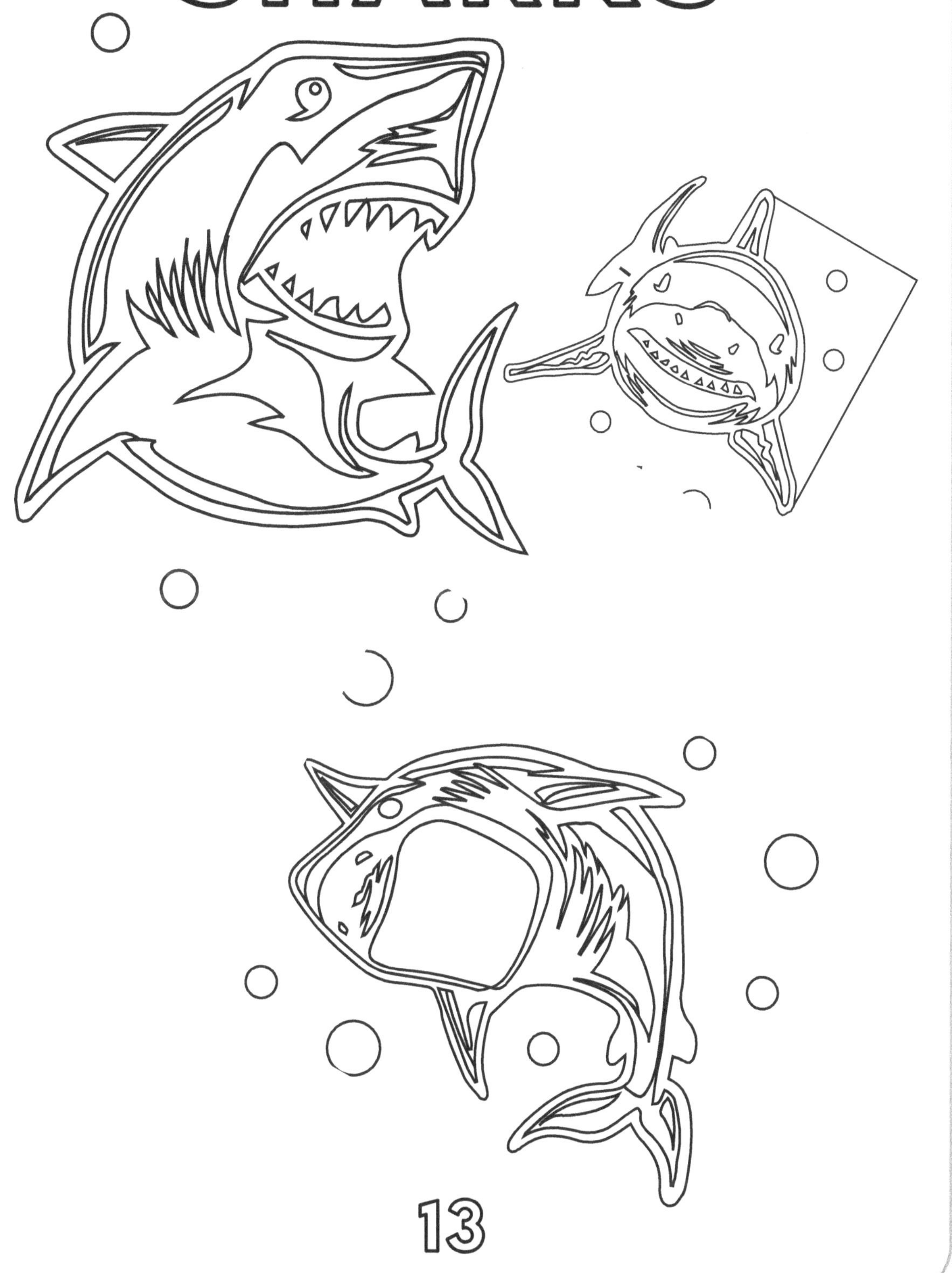

14

TRY TO DRAW A PLOWING FROM THE PREVIOUS PAGE

TURTLE

16

STARFISH

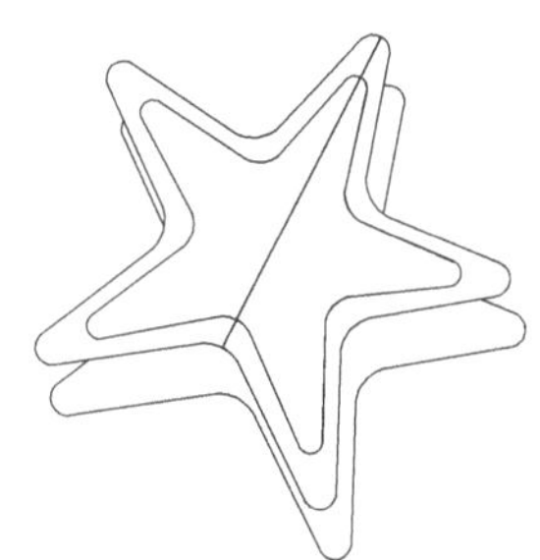

SEASHELL

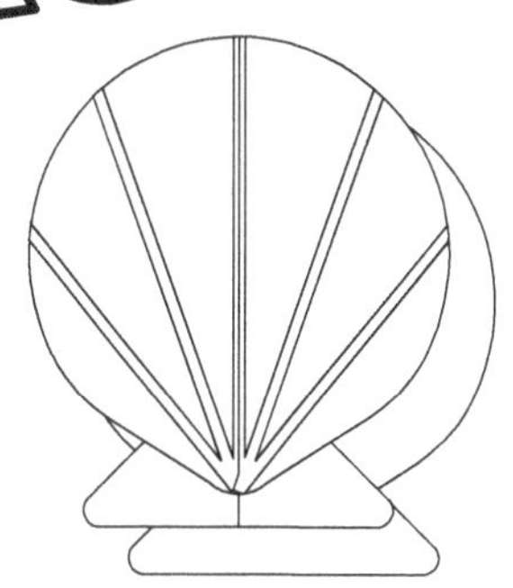

CRAB

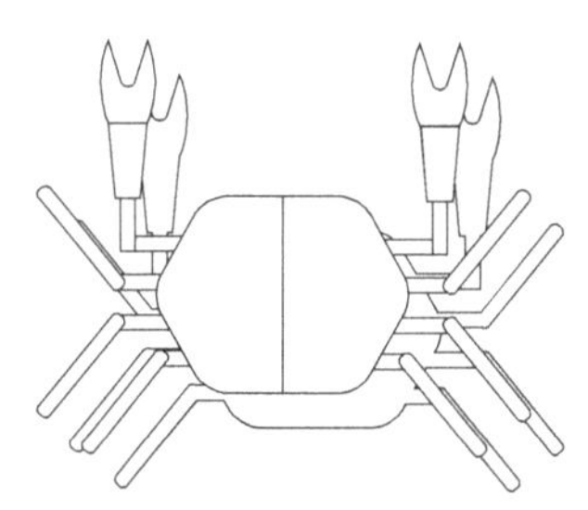

JELLYFISH

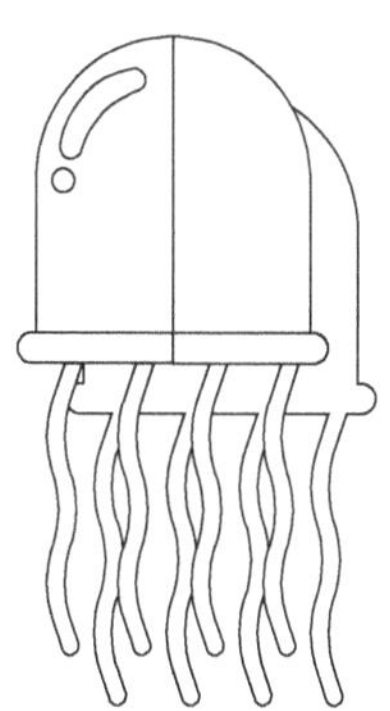

color it

color it

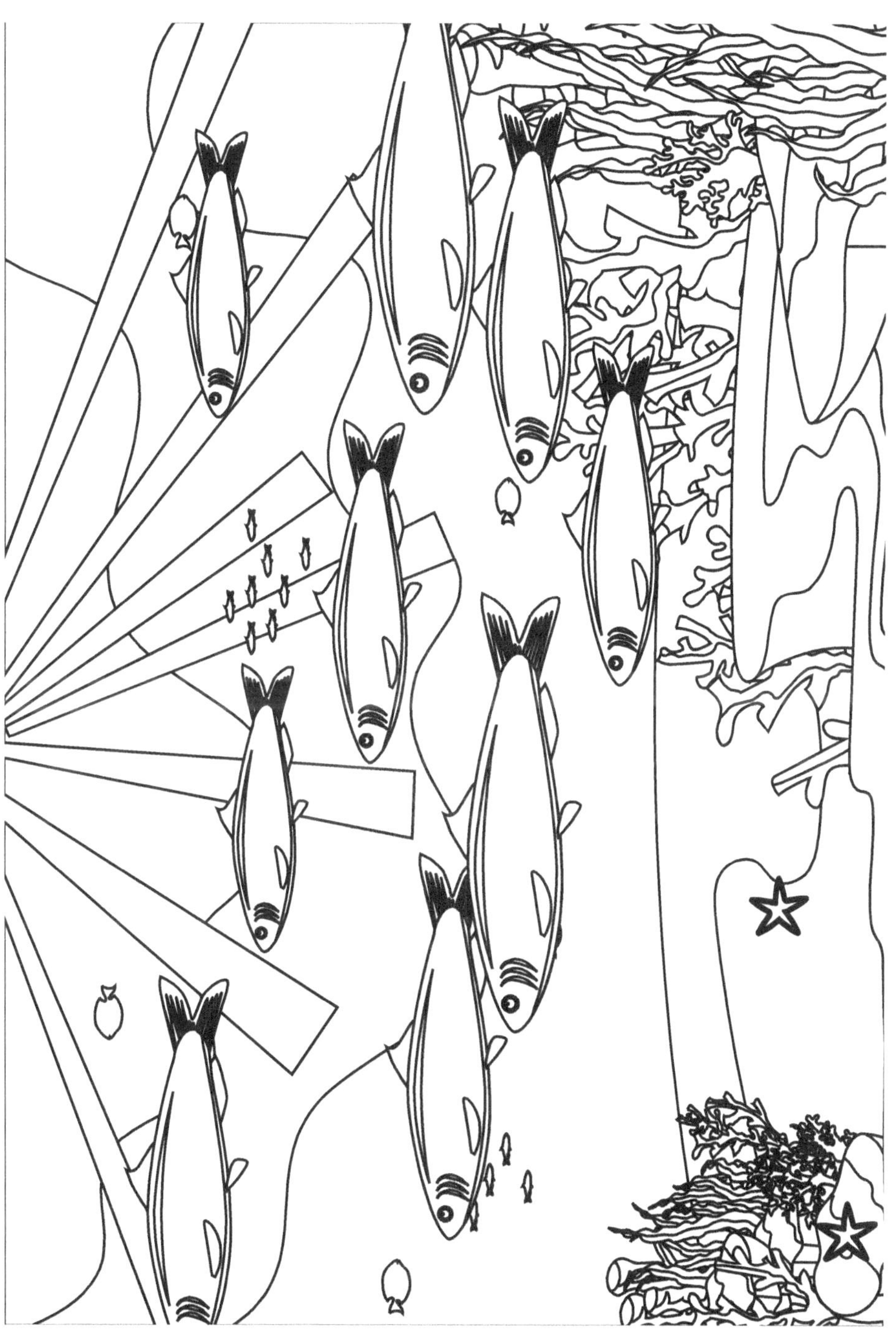

19

Underwater View

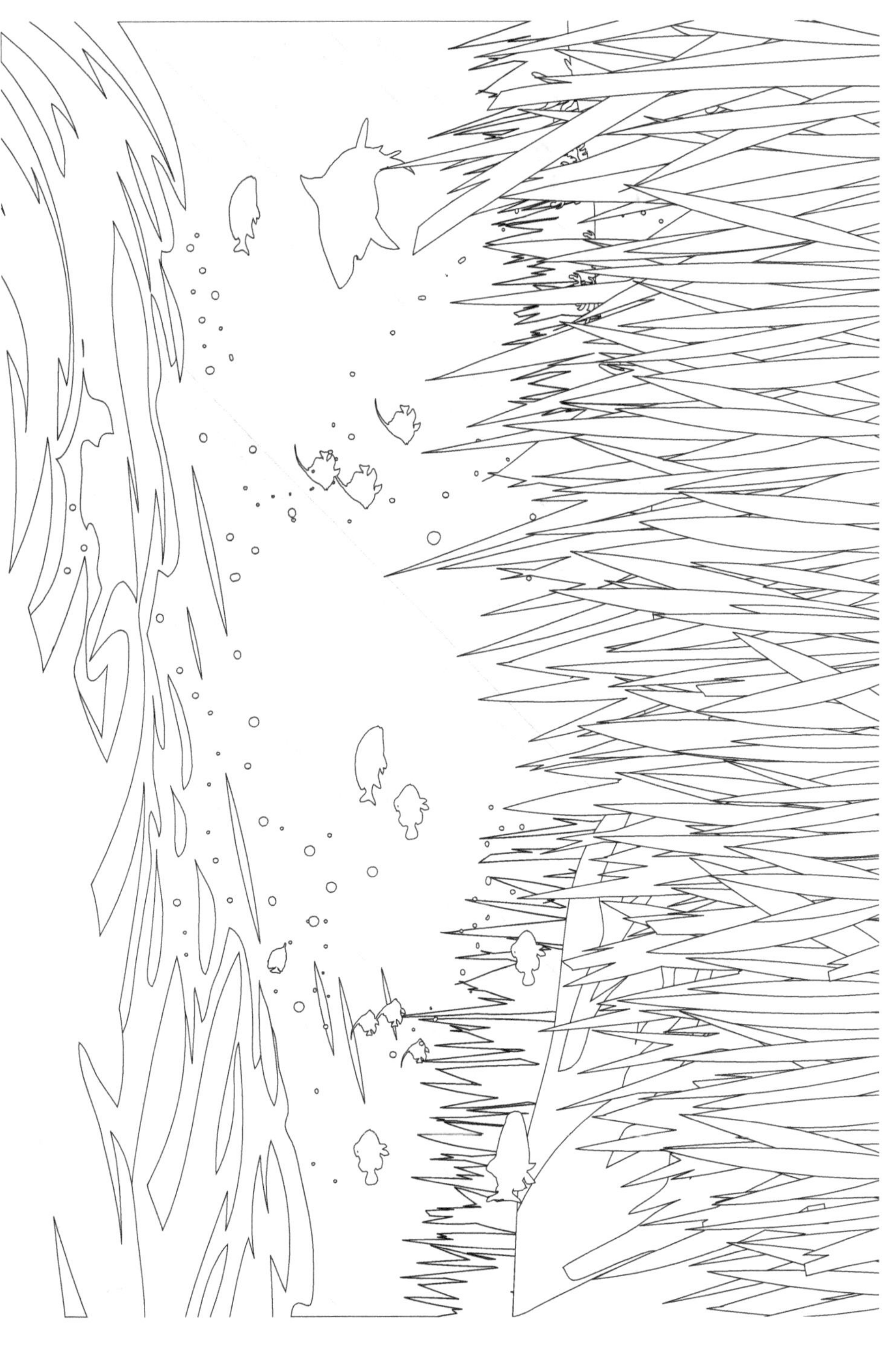

20

SEA PLANTS

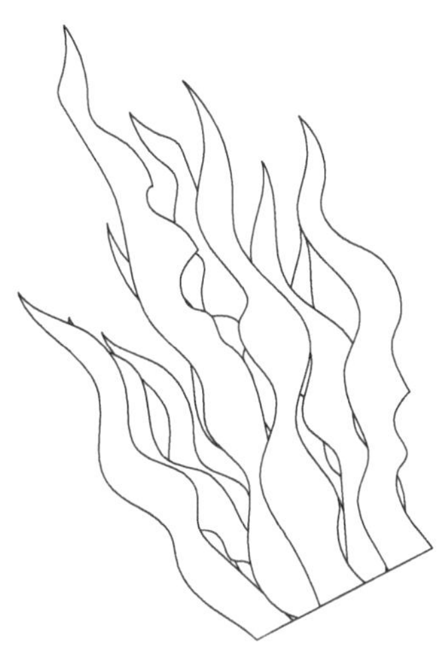

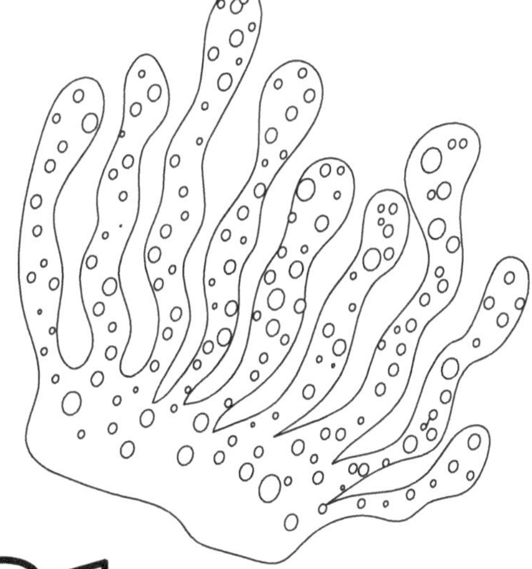

21

SEA PLANTS

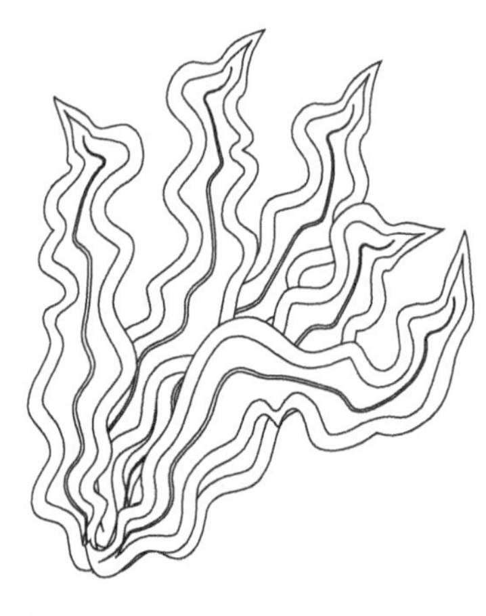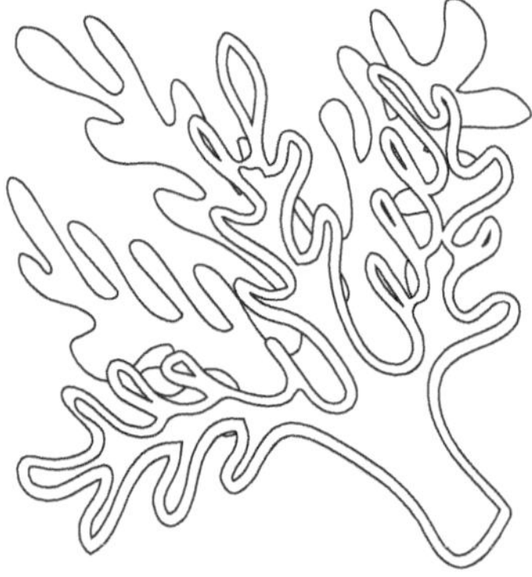

TRY TO DRAW SEA PLANTS FROM THE PREVIOUS PAGE

color it

color it

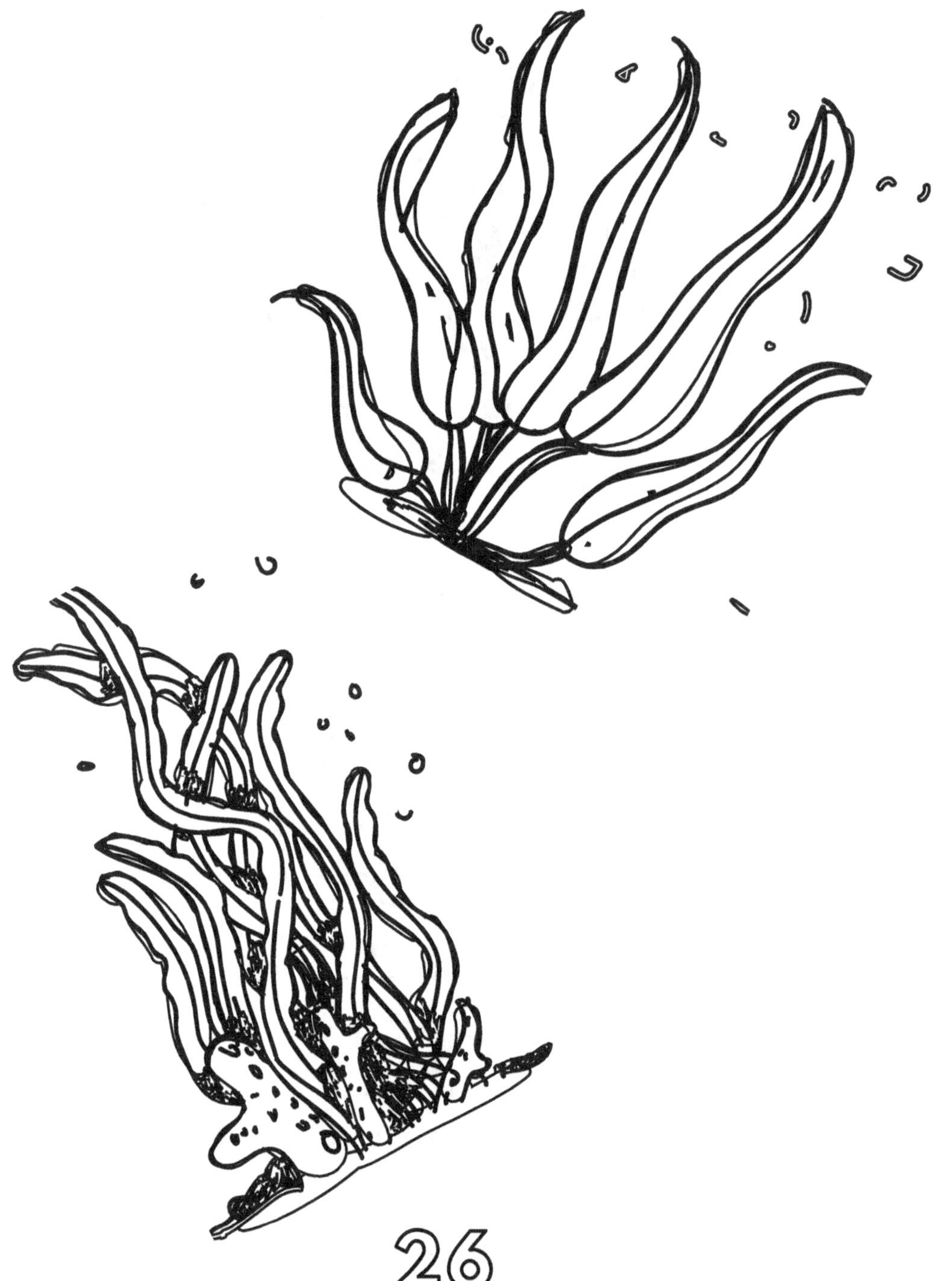

26

TRY TO DRAW SEA
PLANTS FROM THE
PREVIOUS PAGE

color it

Underwater World

28

Color These Castle Gates

30

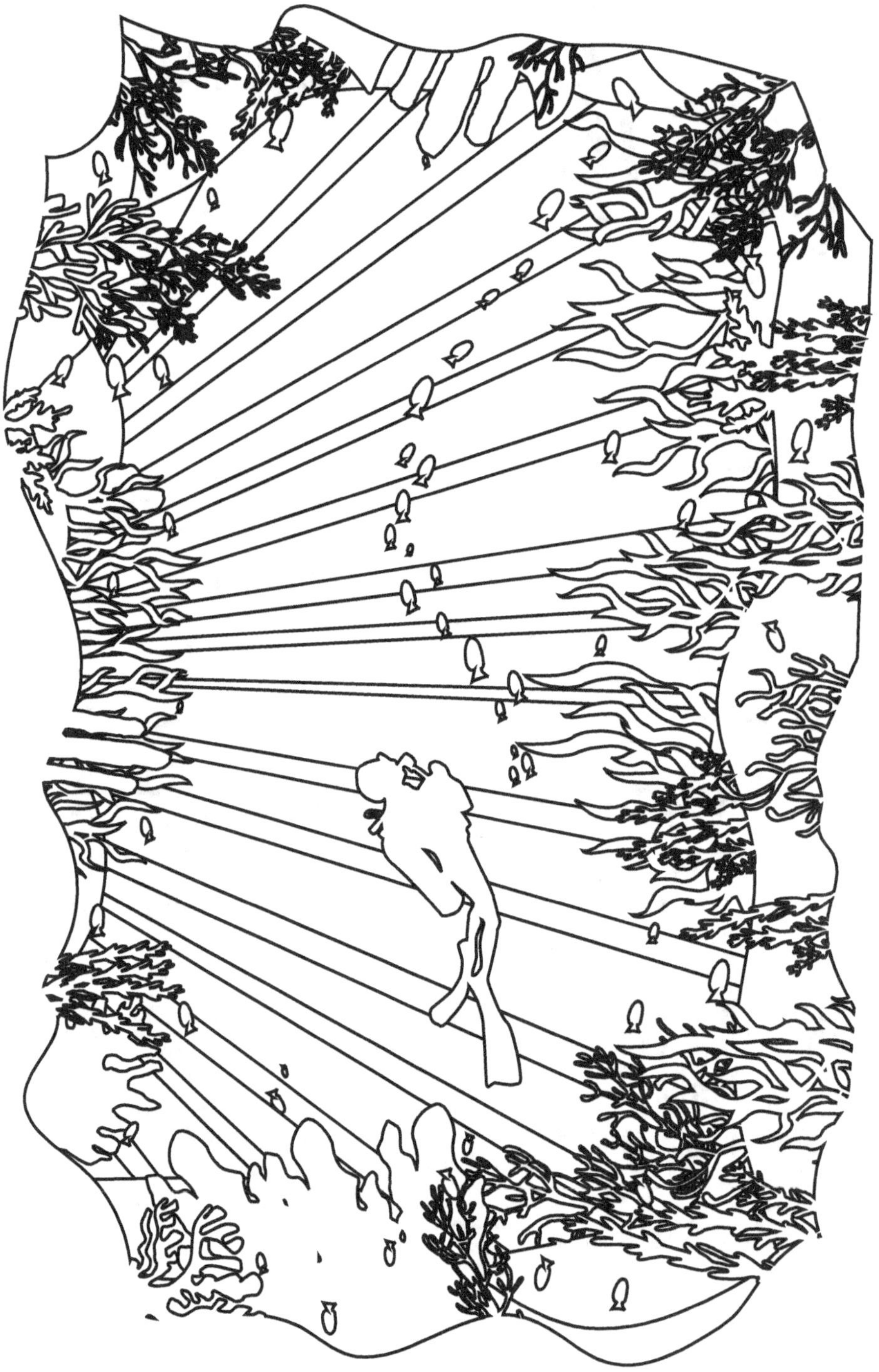

Color it

Repeat These Pictures

Color it

Color it

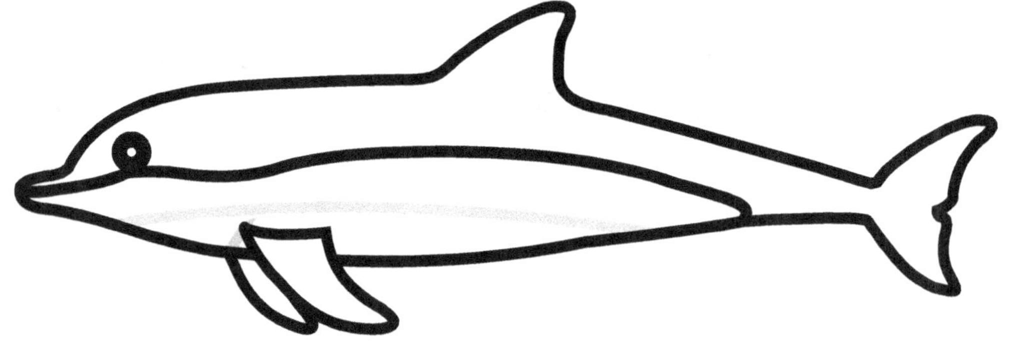

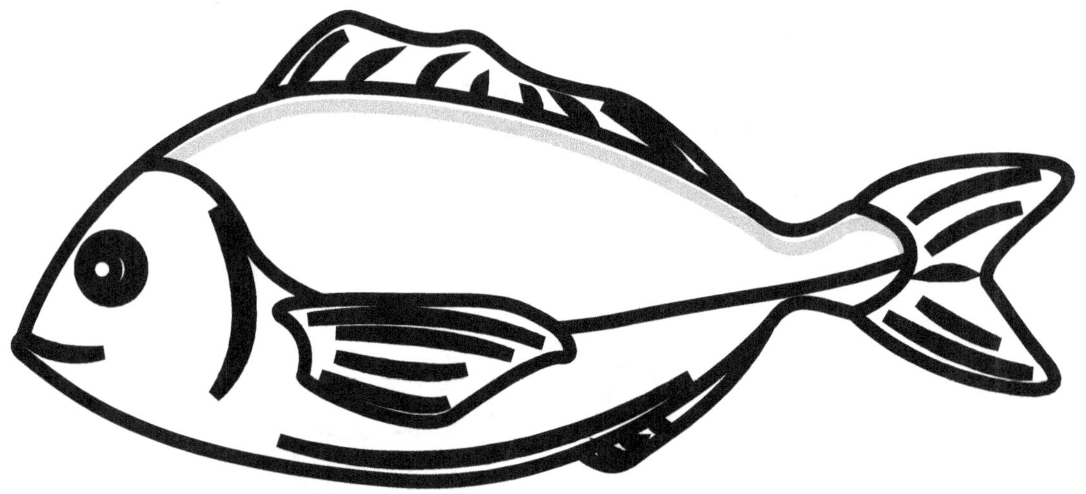

Repeat These Pictures

Color it

Repeat These Pictures

37

38

Repeat These Pictures

Color this Octopus

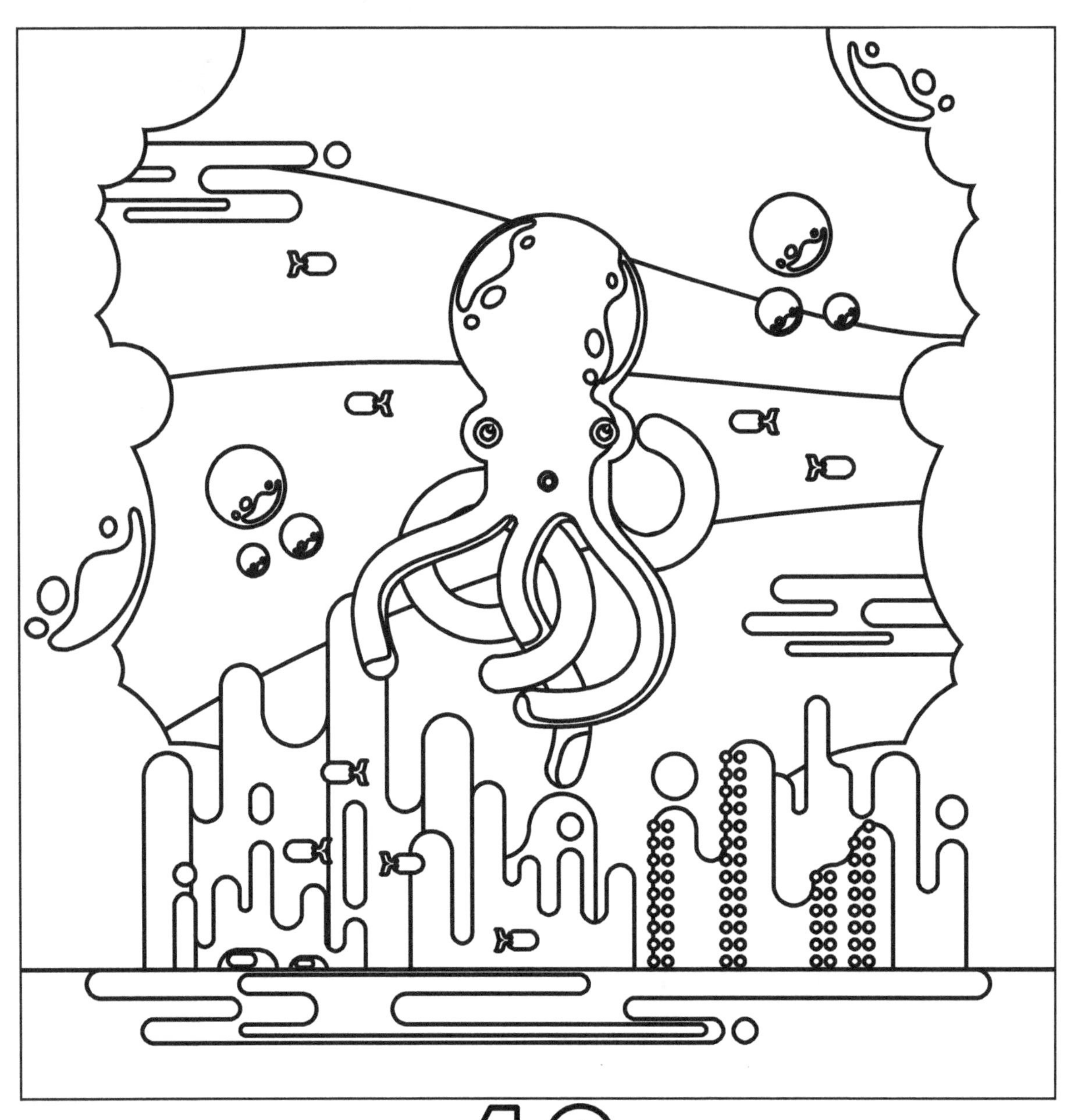

40

41

42

Repeat These Pictures

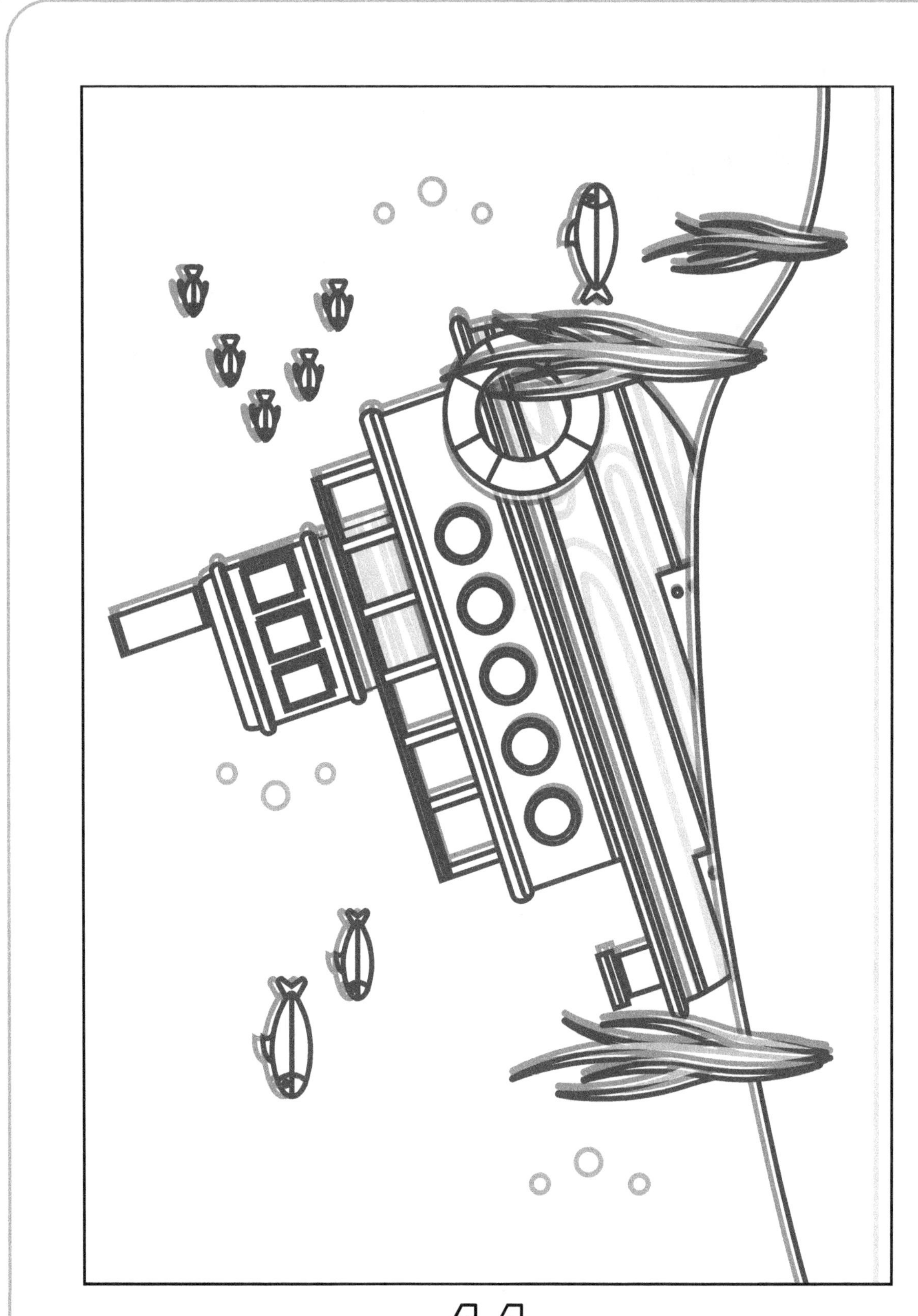

45

TRY TO DRAW SHIP FROM THE PREVIOUS PAGE

COLOR THIS

PICTURE

47

COLOR THESE

FISH

Repeat These Pictures

COLOR THESE

FISH

www.ingramcontent.com/pod-product-compliance
Lightning Source LLC
Chambersburg PA
CBHW080045260726
48658CB00007B/2751